FINALLY A BROKER

Open Your Own Real Estate Office

By

Ricki Eichler McCallum

FINALLY A BROKER

Open Your Own

Real Estate Office

RICKI EICHLER MCCALLUM

DEDICATION

Dedicated to all those who believe
in the American dream and that hard work
and self-sacrifice will return great rewards.

ACKNOWLEDGEMENTS

Thank you to all the people who have invested their time, talent and effort in helping to make this book possible whether it was advice, recommendations, knowledge, or skills. Your contributions in my life and in the writing of this book does not go without sincere appreciation.

A special thank you to Brian Tracy who has been an inspiration to me for several years. His great understanding of the business world and his motivating sales techniques has helped me tremendously.

Thank you to my favorite instructor, Pat Strong. It has been a pleasure sitting in your classes and I highly recommend your coaching to everyone in the real estate business. You have been a source of knowledge unequalled. I thank you from the bottom of my heart.

A very big Thank You goes to Morris Gresham, author and editor; a man I have always looked up to and one that gave me incentive to finish this book and to write more. Morris is my cousin and unfortunately succumbed to cancer before I finished this book. He is looking down on me and proud that I listened to him and finally finished. He will always be my inspiration!

Thanks to all the people who have come and gone throughout the years in my real estate office. From agents to clients, the stories, the experiences, the transactions, good and bad, it has been most memorable.

And Thank You to my wonderful family who provides inspiration and love throughout the writing process!

Thank you to my new audience for reading my first book. The next one will be coming soon.

PREFACE

This book is written for the real estate agent that finally obtained a real estate broker's license or someone working toward that goal that wants to open their own real estate office. Many agents dream for years of being their own boss, of running an office, conducting sales meetings, training others, leading a team of agents to successful careers, and building a solid reputation in the community.

It can take years to get a broker's license in Texas and every agent with the desire to be a broker has to work hard to get the training and also learn the business. Texas requires agents to work in the business and close a certain number of transactions before they can take the license exam.

Brokers also have a responsibility to supervise their agents and there is a course that is mandatory concerning this. A broker is responsible for the actions of their agents and must be knowledgeable and experienced to handle the unique situations that happen every day.

Owning your own real estate office is challenging but can be very lucrative too. **There are many reasons to open an office** *and this book asks you the questions you need to answer before you take this leap.*

You need to ask the right questions if you want to get the right answers.

I have shared stories of my experiences throughout my 40 year career. Hopefully, they will help you to understand the business better and keep you from making the same mistakes I made. Experience is a good teacher. I share the good points and the bad points of owning your own office. It is better to know ahead of time what you are facing than to be caught unaware. I wish you all the success in the world and hope you love real estate like I do. It is my passion!

Ricki Eichler McCallum

Table Of Contents

Chapter 1   A Look Back and Why

Chapter 2   Evaluating Opportunities

11

3. Your specific branding and marketing
4. Opportunity for recognition

Chapter 3   Finding the ideal location

A. Leases
B. Traffic patterns, growth potential
C. Nearby neighborhoods
D. Easy access and visibility
E. The virtual office

Chapter 4   Business Plan

A. Writing your business plan
B. Long term and Short term goals

Chapter 5   Financing

A. Banks
B. Private Lenders
C. Using your own Cash
D. Partnerships

Chapter 6   Agents

A.   A few well trained agents vs. all you can hire
B.   Commission splits

Chapter 7   Staff

A.   Who answers the phone?
B.   Checklists
C.   Policies and procedures-E & O

Chapter 8   Expert Recommendations

A.   Brian Tracy, International Author, Speaker and Business Consultant
B.   Pat Strong, TREC certified instructor
C.   Legal Advice

Chapter 9   The BIG Questions

A.   Why, What, Where, How & When
B.   Client Communication
C.   You Are The Boss

Chapter 1

A Look Back and Why

It was August 1981. The Texas summer sun was beating down on my windshield as I sat in my car in front of the post office. I had just picked up my mail. Yes, the weather was hot but I could not wait to get home to open this letter, I had to open it now! The return address was from Austin, Texas. It was the letter I had been waiting for. It was the answer. Had I passed my broker's exam and was a license in the mail to me? Or had I failed the test and would I have to repeat the process?

The perspiration was dripping from my brow and my hands were shaking as I ripped the envelope open. Unfolding the letter, praying out loud for positive results, so hoping this would be the beginning of my dreams coming true.

It had been almost three years since I had started my real estate career. I had won sales competitions and had studied hard to learn all I could. I had given it my all but I knew it was time to be a broker and be out on my own. I wanted it so badly! I was willing to try and try again until I got that broker's license. I knew I would never stop trying because I wanted it so. It was my passion. It was what I wanted to do in life.

Real estate was the best thing that had ever happened to me. It was fun. It was challenging. It was filled with unlimited potential. I knew it could take me places I wanted to go and give me the life I had always wanted to live.

Now, here in my hands, I held the answer. Would it start today? Or would I have to wait even longer. The sponsoring broker I had was not what I wanted. Being subject to another person's way of running an office was not what I wanted for my career.

The time had come for me to be my own Broker!

Quickly, I read each sentence. Then, halfway down the page it read, "Passed!"

I yelled out loud. So happy! I was crying and my feet were bouncing up and down on the floor board of my car. I was so excited. People passing by, coming and going into the post office were staring at me. I wanted to tell the world,

"I'm Finally a Broker!!!!"

Calming myself as much as I could, I drove home quickly to tell my family and friends. **My dream is coming true!**

A. The "Whys"

"WHY" do you want to own your own real estate office?

There are numerous reasons to own your own office and these can be different for each individual but before you go any farther, it is imperative for you to answer this question for yourself. It is important to know what will drive you past all the obstacles that will come your way. What will give you the motivation to stay in the business when things get tough? You need to answer this question now so you can come back and lean heavily on these thoughts from time to time. IT WILL renew your passion and you will find strength in knowing "why" you started your own office in the first place.

B. Non-Monetary Rewards

Every agent and broker knows about non-monetary rewards in real estate. When you help a first time homebuyer buy their first home, you know that special feeling. It is like nothing else you have ever felt. You know your clients' lives will be different, and better because of the work you did. You know they might never have realized the thrill of home ownership if you had not helped them. You know your work was meaningful and will never be forgotten by these clients. They will forever be grateful. A job well done, with so much self satisfaction will linger in your memory and theirs. Your confidence will be built with each transaction. This is why many Real Estate Agents stay in the business and love what they do. People helping people in a way nobody else can. This is true job satisfaction.

———

I remember a young couple from Florida that wanted to come to Texas. There was a job promotion in store for them if they moved. They were first time homebuyers and neither one of them knew much about home ownership. I spent a lot of time on the phone with them and on the internet guiding them looking at homes in every way we could.

I helped them get pre-approved for a loan and they were sending documents to the lender well ahead of their trip to Texas. They could not afford a very expensive home and could not travel back and forth from Florida. So we had to do everything in advance of their trip to Texas. Securing loan approval and looking at internet photos and descriptions of homes saved time. When they arrived here, we found the home they had been dreaming of, secured a contract, ordered inspections, negotiated repairs, finished the loan, and closed in a relatively short period of time.

We had a time deadline as they were staying in a motel during all of this. There was a small refrigerator and a microwave but eating three meals a day in a motel room was not exactly comfortable. A few dinners out and a few extra meals cooked by me helped them know I was the right agent for them.

Sometimes, your heart goes out to people and you will do all kinds of things for them that are not really part of the job description. This was one such case.

I felt like they were my own children. I would want someone to help my children if they were in the same situation.

Closing day came and they were so excited. Giving them the keys to that darling little house was the best feeling I had all year long.

There were tears and smiles and such joy! You can't get paid enough to replace moments like this. Every REALTOR® knows this feeling.

The young lady hugged me and thanked me numerous times, telling me how they could not have done this without my help. They were so thankful. They gave me beach towels from Florida and a cute plaque with my name on it. It hangs in my office today. She called me her "Angel" from then on.

Non-monetary rewards do count.

1. Be Your Own Boss

Maybe you just want to be your own boss. Entrepreneurial individuals do not like working under the authority of others. They often tend to excel in thinking "outside the box" and have different ideas than their current bosses in operating a business. They want the opportunity to do it their way.

Most entrepreneurial type people do function at a faster rate when strategizing and implementing new ideas. Working for someone else can be frustrating when that person does not make decisions as quickly as you would like.

Are you an entrepreneurial type person?

There are many quizzes and surveys on the internet that can help you answer this question, if there is any doubt in your mind. Most business owners I have talked with have told me their friends and relatives helped them to see the leadership qualities they held long before they decided to become a business owner themselves. That said, remember, your friends and relatives may suggest your new business owner role at first but may later be very negative about you fulfilling this role. A leader of a company, the broker, the owner, must know deep inside they are ready and able to accomplish their goals. Owning and operating a real estate office is very challenging but also very rewarding.

———

I knew at an early age, I was the entrepreneurial type. I was always thinking of ways to make money. I also wanted to own my own business. Whatever I was involved in, I always gave it my all. I would think about the job, the project, the hobby, whatever it was, day and night. I would try to find ways to improve my performance and the performance of others. I would try to lead my friends even as a child in various pursuits. I was the teacher when we played school. I was the judge when we played court. I brought to order the meetings of the newly formed neighborhood clubs. Knowing I was like this, it was not hard for me to figure out I was the entrepreneurial type. It came naturally.

———

You may not think you have this natural desire and ability. However, that does not mean you will not succeed. You just have to know what you want and have the passion to go get it no matter what! Passion is always the key. So, do it!

2. Recognition

Is recognition really that important? No, not in the light of the rewards of a job well done, that leads a family into a whole new lifestyle with the purchase of a new home. However, recognition is a great benefit that comes from being a business owner. Broker/owners are looked at in the community as the real experts in the housing market. The local realty boards look to the broker/owners for leadership for the whole agent populace. There are more opportunities to grow your business and other business ventures at the same time. In your position as broker/owner, opportunities will come your way. The public has an insatiable appetite for all things real estate. It is the key to opening many conversations with people you want to know.

If you have been a real estate agent for a period of time, sold properties and finally earned enough credits scholastically to take your test for your broker's license, passed your test, received your broker's license, you may be ready to open your own office.

Before you do, let's continue to look at the opportunities and obstacles that may be in your way.

3. Helping Others

"Helping Others" is something most brokers do without hesitation.   This is one of the things that lead and keep many agents in the real estate field. Being directly responsible for helping a family get a good deal on a home, knowing it will bring stability in that family, build equity for their clients and fulfill their housing needs.

Another way of helping others is training agents to be successful and this is the role of a good broker/owner. There is deep satisfaction that comes from teaching an agent how to help others also. When that agent closes a first time homebuyer, everyone wins. The buyer, the agent, the broker are all benefited in ways more than just financially.

Realtors® benefit their communities with more than just home sales. They take part in educating the public on new laws, on issues that relate to land development, taxes, natural resources, home ownership, and so much more. Realtors® provide valuable services to the public, many times without compensation.

Watching your agents grow as professionals and knowing you were a part of their success and how that success impacts the lives of their families and countless other families that are clients of your agents is like a pat on your back. Everyone wants to feel their job has helped people and communities. As a broker/owner you have this wonderful opportunity.

C. Potential Earnings and Profits

Potential Earnings and Profits is the biggest reason for owning your own real estate office. Being able to keep all of your commission on every sale you make instead of giving some to the company that has previously sponsored you is one of the things most brokers consider first. It is the strongest motivator for anyone preparing to take their broker's exam. Secondly, the opportunity of sponsoring other agents and receiving part of their commission is another big reason to own your own office. I put this reason last in the list because I do not want you to overlook the other reasons. Of course, money is the first motivator, but when things get tough, you will find the other reasons more valuable to you.

Spend time calculating what the potential income can be for you and your company based on what you are now making in sales without sharing your commissions with another agency. Project what other agents might bring into your business. The more agents you have will usually mean more sales and more profits. However, not all agents produce at the same rate and you must try to forecast their performance by looking at statistics of other agencies in your area.

Next, make a list of all the expenses you will incur when you start a real estate office. What will be the monthly expenses due every month? What will be expenses that come due only once a year? The real estate business has lots of yearly expenses like dues and fees from local, state and national boards. MLS dues are usually paid quarterly as are payroll taxes. Take time to figure everything that might be an expense. Get help from another broker/business owner or from your CPA. Make a spreadsheet and include *rent, utilities, advertising, printing, office supplies, office furniture, equipment, computer services, janitorial, car expenses, gasoline, telephones, and so much more*. Don't forget smaller expenses like refreshments for office meetings, parties, open houses. All this adds up quickly.

I am sure you have had a lot of these same expenses as an agent. When you open an office of your own, the expenses multiply quickly. As we will discuss in later chapters, agent incentives can move the profit margin greatly in both directions. Balancing expenses profits is where your expertise will determine the success of your company.

Look at this carefully and consider the "what ifs". There are many "what ifs" that can occur and do more often than not. Preparing in advance is always the best way. Surprises in expenses or income can be devastating to any business but especially in real estate. Never count on a commission until it is in your bank account.

Real estate offices operate on commissions only just like a real estate agents' business. Some months are better than others. When working just by yourself you can manage the expenses easier and pull back when necessary, but when you have an office with agents the expenses are ongoing. You cannot stop the cost of printing, advertisements or utilities. Plan appropriately and give yourself room for the unexpected.

D. Your Answer

At the beginning of this chapter, you were asked to decide "why" you wanted to start your own real estate office. After looking at several different reasons, have you decided which apply to you? Are there others? Write these down. Keep a copy of the "Whys" in a convenient place for quick reference. Read the answers and renew your passion for your business when you become discouraged. There will be those times. A very wise lady, a business owner for 40 plus years, once told me, "The secret to success is in the STAYING POWER."

This simple sentence has penetrated my thinking many times and given me the strength to go on when times were tough. When people don't appreciate you, when the expenses are too much, when sales are down, when you are tired and you feel overwhelmed, think about this sentence.

"The secret to success is in the STAYING POWER."

That's what Mrs. Braswell told me. She was a longtime business owner and friend I admired very much.

Sometimes the best lessons we learn are those that we never experience ourselves but that someone else shares with us. Hopefully, you will reap a good lesson from this book that will save you from making the same mistakes I have already made. We learn from one another.

CHAPTER 2

Evaluating Opportunities

In this chapter we will look at the opportunities that are currently present in your marketplace.   Buying a pre-existing office in operation may be easier than starting a new office. There are advantages in both. Let's examine the differences.

Existing Offices in Operation

1. Owner Financing

Buying an existing business of any kind but especially real estate offices, usually has one particular advantage. That advantage is easy owner financing. In the beginning of any career or business venture, securing funds to purchase can be a major hurdle to overcome. With owner financing, you can skip the lengthy qualifying process and possibly obtain a mentor at the same time. Sellers want to know they will get their money and they will often help the new owner with training and other support to ensure the success of the new owner/broker.

If you use a business broker to find an office, they will have all the information you need already available concerning what terms the seller may offer. The interest rates can vary from very high to even better than a bank would offer. The reason for this is the owner not only will get his price for the business but get interest on a monthly basis as well. The seller has another advantage in offering owner financing because of income taxes at the end of the year. If a business is financed over a period of years, the seller only pays for what he has received in any given year. Therefore, the tax bill is lower. This is a big reason why owner financing is sometimes available.

Owner financing can work well for the new buyer as well as for the seller. Many businesses are sold each year utilizing owner financing. Do not be afraid to ask for different terms if necessary. Some sellers are anxious and you may find a really good deal.

2. Reputation

Reputation means a lot in the real estate field. A good name that implies good service over a length of time is invaluable. The seller has advertised in various ways including every sign that sat in someone's yard. Every time someone else drove by and saw that sign, this company received image recognition. The community is familiar with the company name, the service, the staff, and the agents. This kind of reputation will save you time in getting listings and sales rather than having to build your reputation one sale at a time.

As we will discuss later, advertising takes time for clients to recognize. Advertising is one of your largest expenses. If you buy an existing business, you are reaping the rewards of years of advertising expense the seller has spent.

The existing office staff, agents and broker have most likely spent much time in promoting the business during community functions. Being a part of any community and being well known for charitable deeds will bring in business. These are part of the reasons you should look into currently operating offices that are for sale in your area.

3.Existing Clientele

Another benefit of buying an existing office is past and present clientele. In an existing office, there will be listings already on the market. This is like money in the bank. There can be pending sales that go with the sale of the office. This is your inventory. They often sell with the business.

There are also past clients that will come back to the same company when they need real estate services again. Contacts like this can save a new owner/broker years of work. It could take many years to reach where an existing office already is. Clients do not like to change. If they are happy with an office, they will come back time after time. They will also refer their friends. Referrals are the icing on the cake.

Everything in place is another advantage to buying the existing office. Signs, logos, business cards, advertising materials, policies and procedures, forms, furniture, equipment, insurance are just some of the things you will have to have in order to do business. An existing office has all this in place and the cost of buying all this in an existing office is usually minimal compared to creating it all over again. Buying an existing office is something you should seriously consider.

New Start-up

1. New image and excitement

A new start-up office can have a new look, new image, fresh ideas that the marketplace will embrace. New businesses always bring excitement. Never underestimate the power of excitement. Excitement is contagious and can be used as the best agent recruiter available. Excitement brings new listings and listings that did not previously sell with a different agency. Your community, your Chamber of Commerce, local civic clubs always rally behind new offices. Some will even provide free advertising to help you get started.

Depending on where you live, you may want to take advantage of local history, trends, or landmarks to brand your office. Another idea is to use your name in your branding. If you decide to do this, remember, one day you may want to sell the business. Will it sell easy with your name on it? Weigh this decision carefully.

Your local Chamber of Commerce will be a good place to start to publicize your new office. They may offer a ribbon cutting for new businesses also. The newspaper and local magazines will run press releases free of charge or for a small fee. They will look forward to your future advertising money.

A website is a must and the internet offers a wide audience for it. The look of your website and the ease of navigating it will be a big part of your business. Don't skimp on this with time or money.

I have been told many times my website was so easy to navigate that people who were buying from another company actually used my website because it was easy to understand and find what they were looking for. Your website will tell the world who you are and what your company does. The more information you provide, the more service you offer to your clients. Your reputation may start here.

Remember, not everyone has good eyesight either. Make your website and all of your marketing easy to see and read.

2. Your own policies and procedures

Having the opportunity to put your own policies and procedures in place can be an advantage for many broker/owners. Everyone has their own way of things. With a start-up company you will make the decisions about what processes will be used and in what manner. There will be lots of decisions to make but if you enjoy doing this, do it! I found in my own office, there were many more policies than laws to follow. My agents would just laugh and say, "It's the policy of this office..."

We will discuss policies and procedures manuals in further detail in Chapter 7. Your manual is updated frequently from Realtor® associations and you can add to it also.

3. Your specific branding and marketing

Want to "brand" your office with a specific logo, design, image or style? A new start-up company allows you to do that. While an existing company already has logos and branding in place, the start-up can be anything you like. Be creative. Take the time to plan your branding. Don't be hasty. Ask friends and relatives to give you feedback about your ideas of branding. Remember, this is one thing you cannot change. It is too expensive to advertise and get public recognition and then change to something totally different. Be sure the first time. If you are not creative and do not know what images, pictures, or words you should use, hire a company that does this sort of thing. It will not be as expensive as it will be if you do it wrong. Again, this is something you cannot change once you've made the decisions about branding.

Advertising is everything in real estate. The marketing of listings does not begin until after you have marketed your company image. Image advertising is a large expense and you cannot judge the results as easy as advertising your listings and watching them sell as you advertise them. Some brokers fail to do image advertising but it is as important as advertising for a sale. A strong image will get listings. Listings will get sales.

Sales make you successful. It all starts with advertising--- marketing and branding. Advertising may be your largest expense.

4. Opportunity for Recognition

Recognition of your accomplishments from business leaders comes faster when you start your own company. Buying an existing company and keeping it successful takes hard work but starting a new office is much harder. Business leaders know this and will recognize you for it.   Your career path can leap forward much faster when leaders know it was your expertise, planning and hard work that created a new business.

Recognition is very important for some people. It is the force that motivates some to get out of bed every day and to do their best. If you are one to reach for perfection because of the recognition, you are a driven person and rewards, bonuses, and other forms of recognition are a means of self-motivation. You love the competition and you will look for others to partner with that have the same drive.

Do not be afraid of recognition. You must promote yourself and your company. It is not wrong to seek to be the best and it is not wrong to let people know you are the best!

These are just some of the things to consider when comparing the possibility of buying an existing business to starting a new one. There may not be an existing business in your area for sale or there may be more than one. Check with business brokers. They often do not advertise offices for sale as their clients require lots of privacy. Compare the costs of start-up with an existing business. Which one is the better opportunity for you? Weigh the risks. Which one is the better fit? Which one will motivate you more?

———

A quick note about **FRANCHISES:** Franchises offer a real boost to the owner/broker with big name recognition. They also offer all the branding materials you will need. However, they are quite expensive. There is a big fee at the beginning and then monthly or yearly fees from then on. Your location in the county or state will determine how much you need a franchise. The larger the area, the bigger the competition and the more a franchise may help you. With that being said, understand that independent brokerages far outnumber franchise offices. If you are in a big city, the franchise is a bigger advantage than it is in a small town usually.

Chapter 3

Finding the Ideal Location

How important is location? Have you ever heard that old saying? *"Location, location, location"*

Location is all important. People must be able to find you. There must be easy access and visibility in and out of your parking lot. If you are buying an existing office, location may not be an issue. If the business has been successful in the past, location may be right and you might want to stay there. If things have not been as good as you think they could be, then a move might be in order.

A. Leases

When buying an existing office or beginning a start-up, chances are you will need to lease a location.   Leases can be tricky. Too long a term is just as bad as too short a term. The longer the term usually means the better price per month, however. Check all the clauses of a lease carefully. Have your attorney read it if you are not familiar with commercial leases. Know what other things you will be required to pay for with a lease. Taxes, insurance, maintenance, lawn care, lighting, locks, signage, fire equipment, and the list goes on. If you are not aware of some of the extra expenses, it can cut into your budget and make your business much less profitable.

B. Traffic Patterns, Growth Potential

Traffic patterns and growth potential is worth investigating. A good location today could become a not so desirable location in the future. If roads were diverted or even closed, your business could become invisible to the passing traffic. Checking with the state highway department is a good idea when considering a location. Find out what the future traffic patterns will look like in that area in years to come. The highway department has all kinds of statistical information that can be very valuable to you. Traffic counts in an area can show increasing or decreasing business patterns. Of course, you want to be where the business will grow and be most profitable.

The highway department can most likely provide you with information about growth potential as well. The Chamber of Commerce is also a good source for information.   Talk to everyone and don't be afraid to ask questions. Planning for your future location is essential to success.

If there are highway improvements or changes coming to the area you are planning to locate to, find out how long the construction process will take. This construction time can be detrimental to any business. One time, I opened a business and within a year, the highway department began construction on the highway in front of my business. I had not planned for this when I opened the business. The construction took longer than expected. At one point, there was a thirty foot high pile of gravel in the driveway to my business. Nobody could come in or out. Fortunately, I had a second entrance in the rear but it almost stopped all customer traffic and I suffered a huge financial loss. I speak from experience about road construction, so be sure to check with the local and state highway departments about any changes they intend to make within a five year period or more of opening your business. Remember, many businesses have closed because of situations like this and it was not the fault of the entrepreneur. The government has more rights than you when it comes to road construction. Plan your location well.

C. Nearby Neighborhoods

Nearby neighborhoods are another thing to consider when planning for a good location for your real estate office. Neighborhoods are the source of your income if you are selling residential real estate. Being located near a popular neighborhood that draws residents to an area can provide your office with ready and accessible leads and listings. Never underestimate the power of being located near a popular neighborhood. One of my best friends in the real estate business, located her office near a neighborhood like this. Her office became the number one producer in her city and she and her agents rarely sold outside of this one neighborhood.

Real estate is about referrals and repeat business. A steady flow of clients from a large popular neighborhood can pay the bills for you. This would allow the other areas you sell in and other kinds of property like commercial to be extra profit. Look at your community. Is there a neighborhood like this where lots of people desire to live? Is it affordable for most? Is there easy access? Is there an opportunity to locate nearby? Are the schools desirable? Will a leased property in this area be within your budget limits? If so, this is definitely a possible location to investigate.

D. Easy Access and Visibility

We have already discussed access and how important it is for your business. Easy access means an easy way to enter the parking lot, navigate the parking lot and leave without encountering highway traffic that is traveling so fast it makes it dangerous to enter or leave your property. Slower speed limits can be a real advantage.

A well designed parking lot will have easy turn around capabilities also. Striping can help and make a small space seem larger.

Visibility is what every business needs. Clients need to be able to see the building on approach in time to turn in. Your signage should be large enough to read from a moving car. This will bring in more revenue. Signage is very important at your location and also in your clients' yards. Make sure you design a logo that is not only interesting and colorful but READABLE. How many times have you seen signs that are not readable? Many, many times is the answer. Signs cost a lot of money to produce but will pay back their cost numerous times over if clients can read them while passing by.

I want to share an advertising tip with you while we are discussing signage. After all, signs are advertising. I learned a long time ago, it takes about seven times for a client to see a sign or an ad and actually be able to recognize it later. This is why it is so important to make your logos and art work readable and understandable. Visibility applies to your building, your location sign, your yard signs, your car signs, your name badges, your letterheads. Everything you do should have the same kind of printing and artwork on it.

Thomas Smith wrote "Successful Advertising" in 1885 and in that guide he listed 20 different ideas that a consumer would have when they saw your advertising. It is quite interesting and is still being used today.

"The first time people look at any given ad, they don't even see it.

The second time, they don't notice it.

The third time, they are aware that it is there.

The fourth time, they have a fleeting sense that they've seen it somewhere before.

The fifth time, they actually read the ad.

The sixth time they thumb their nose at it.

The seventh time, they start to get a little irritated with it.

The eighth time, they start to think, "Here's that confounded ad again."

The ninth time, they start to wonder if they're missing out on something.

The tenth time, they ask their friends and neighbors if they've tried it.

The eleventh time, they wonder how the company is paying for all these ads.

The twelfth time, they start to think that it must be a good product.

The thirteenth time, they start to feel the product has value.

The fourteenth time, they start to remember wanting a product exactly like this for a long time.

The fifteenth time, they start to yearn for it because they can't afford to buy it.

The sixteenth time, they accept the fact that they will buy it sometime in the future.

The seventeenth time, they make a note to buy the product.

The eighteenth time, they curse their poverty for not allowing them to buy this terrific product.

The nineteenth time, they count their money very carefully.

The twentieth time prospects see the ad, they buy what it is offering."

In 1885, people may have needed even more advertising to drive them toward a sale. Twenty times seems like a lot. Today, I believe in the "Rule of Seven". In other words, it takes at least seven times of seeing an ad before you recognize and remember it. So practice continuity in your advertising, whether it is on signs or print or electronic communication it should look the same. Keep your branding in place.

You want your company to be very visible. If you locate in an area where there are 20,000-30,000 cars or more a day that pass by, chances are many of those people are commuting back and forth to work or school and will see your signs twice a day. In a few days, they will have seen your signs seven times and your company will begin to make an impression on people's minds and attitudes. Make sure you cover the view area from both directions.

Make a good impression with the visibility your company holds. Make the entrance inviting. One of the hardest things in opening a new real estate office is getting people to come in. For some reason, people want to avoid coming in to real estate offices. It is the "Fear Factor" that someone will try a hard sell with them. Make sure the impression your office has is friendly and non-threatening.

E. The Virtual Office

The Virtual office is a newer concept. There are many options available with software or with companies that provide complete real estate systems. Some even have virtual buildings and avatars that can go to meetings with other avatars. The field is limitless.

With the opportunities we have today to work at home and to advertise on the internet, the virtual office may suit your needs. It works for many agents that prefer to work in their own homes. Especially, parents who have children at home or anyone that has enough discipline and structure in their lives to avoid the many distractions that come with a home office.

I personally have always worked at home a lot. Even if I put in a full day at a physical location, I will come home and work even longer at home. Working in my pajamas or being able to do some laundry at the same time I am writing contracts is something I have no trouble doing.

Multi-tasking? We really do not multi-task. The washing machine may be running at the same time we are typing but we can only do one thing at a time. One thing has your attention all the time.

Lots of people like to think they can look at their phones and listen at the same time. It really does not work that way. You must focus your attention on what you are doing to be successful. So, if you have a virtual office where you only work at home, put the distractions away. Concentrate on your work and do the same things you would do if you had a physical office location.

Before you decide this is the way to go since it is less expensive, consider the agents you will hire to work in your virtual office. How will you conduct office meetings? How will you keep records? How will you supervise?

Your first office should be the one that works best for YOU. If you are most comfortable with a physical location, get a physical location. If you are most comfortable with a virtual office, choose a good company that offers that option to start with. You will have more fun and be more successful when you choose the one that works best for you.

Chapter 4

Business Plan

A. Writing Your Business Plan

Every successful business owner will need a business plan. Writing your own can be a challenge. You know what you want and need or do you? Get help in writing your business plan. A trusted friend that has successfully done this before or a business owner you admire can help you. Or you may want to get help from professionals. Do not let people without experience advise you or it will be detrimental to your company.

There are some programs on the internet that can also help. A quick Google check will open some opportunities for you. The small business administration offers a lot of help to small businesses also. Check them out at www.sba.gov . One may be what you need.

A business plan is a carefully thought out plan with goals for various stages in the development of your business. It is a projection of expenses and income based on facts and speculation. It is your company's blueprint for growth to summarize operational and financial goals. A good business plan describes who, what, where, when and why your company exists and what it plans to do. Without a business plan, you will not be able to secure the capital it takes to start a new venture.

It's all about the money! Like baking a cake, start with the right recipe. It's the same as in building a home; use blueprints and build a good foundation first. When starting a business, your business plan means everything.

There are traditional business plans that are lengthy with eight or nine key sections. Today, however, many people use a shorter version and incorporate more information in the sections. The first section should be **Executive Summary** and describes your service, potential customers and clients, and future of your company. This can be in a long traditional plan or short version.

The next section is **Company Description**. Again, you can go into detail or not. I recommend being as precise as you can and still give the reader a good view of what your business is really about. You may include your mission statement here. The owners and management team is also listed in this section. Be sure to add the legal structure of the company as well. This is a very important section.

The next section can be **Market Analysis or Research**. Here you will describe who your customers and clients will be. You will also give the reasons why doing business with your company will have advantages.

Section Four can be Services or Products You Offer. Briefly describe all services your company offers. You may or may not want to share pricing structures. That would work better for companies that sell products. In a residential real estate office, you are offering services not products. However, there may be some products you could offer in your office, depending on how it is set up.   Life cycle is the next subset of this section. In other words, how often will you be able to get repeat business from the same customer or client? Referrals from past clients will be figured in this section.

Marketing and Sales should be the next section and here you may discuss a variety of things. Marketing and Sales will be your line of revenue. It will also be your largest expense. I would put follow up and repeat business here also.

Next is the **Funding Request**. If you are borrowing money, you will be putting the figures you need here. Remember, business plans are required to borrow money but having a plan for yourself to follow is also important even if you are not borrowing money.

Last is the **Financial Projections**. Hopefully, these projections will be a realistic projection of your future profits. After you see this, you may or may not decide to open your own office. Do a business plan before anything else.

B. Long Term and Short Term Goals

Your Business Plan should have both, **goals for the short term and goals for the long term.** Let's look at the long term first.

Your banker is most interested in the **long term**, say five years and more. Loans are usually long term and the lenders today are interested in the beginning and the end. They want to know you have a plan that will take your company successfully into the future and be able to repay all loans. Helping lenders to see step by step progression of your business is key to obtaining loans. They must believe your company has a good chance of success or they will not be willing to invest in you. A good idea, a good plan, a good location, good people, good skills, enthusiasm, and the power of persuasion will put the banker on your side.

Short term goals can change quickly and if something is not working, you have the ability to change it and try something different. Short term goals are the ones that motivate you the most when you achieve them. It is easier to take smaller steps than big ones. Take enough small ones and they become a big one. Remember, you will walk a mile one step at a time.

Short term goals will make or break you. You must keep making these short term goals. Never think you don't need to make and keep short term goals simply because you have long term goals in place. The short term goals define you and your company even more. They are the ones that give you the ahhhhs, the smiles on your face at the end of a struggle that turns out in your favor.

Short term goals pay the bills. Week after week, sale after sale, commission after commission, the short term goals are met. They keep us going strong. They motivate, inspire and give us the courage to keep trying. Short term goals are the ones your sales agents will need the most.

Long term goals are for the company as a whole. They are for you, for your future. Most agents will not care about long term goals for the company. They are interested in right now. Find an agent interested in long term goals for your company and you have found a gem. They are few and far between.

Chapter 5

Financing

One of the biggest hurdles you will face in any business startup is the financing. There are several ways you can go.

A. Banks

Banks love to lend money to small businesses and even startup companies if they have a good business plan and good support. If you have dealt with your banking institution in the past and have a good rapport with your personal banker, you have a good chance of obtaining the money you need.

Before you sign the loan documents however, comparison shop the loan just like you would shop for a car or for furniture. Different banks can offer entirely different rates. Compare; don't just take the first offer you get. A difference in interest rate can make the difference in whether you succeed or not.

If your local banks do not meet your needs, consider the SBA. SBA loans are competitive in the marketplace. They do require more paperwork and a longer time period to obtain. They go through a local bank but are guaranteed by the government and that always means more paperwork. If you are a minority class, there may even be some incentives for you.

B. Private Lenders

The second way of obtaining cash is private lenders. There are many of these waiting to invest in your company. Finding the right one is the hard part. There are advertisements in many newspapers and on the internet for private lenders.

There may be some that have store fronts in your city also. I know of a private lender in a nearby city that does loans for real estate every day. The president of the company says, "If it makes sense, we will do it." He loves to say that and every time I talk to him, I hear that phrase several times before the conversation ends. I have sent many clients to him for loans. The interest rates are a little higher than with a bank and the application fee is also, but the paperwork is less, the time to process is less as well. It makes sense in many situations.

One of the best ways to find a good private lender or investor is to ask your CPA who they know that has some money they want to invest. Some people look for investment opportunities toward the end of the year. Don't pass up an opportunity by not asking people you know.

Word of caution: check out the lenders you are considering using. Lenders are so numerous and some are unscrupulous as we have seen in the recent past with all the loans that were made to people who did not qualify. A good lender will provide you with all the answers you need if you ask. Do not be pressured into a loan you feel uncomfortable about. Remember, that loan has to be paid back and payback is not as easy as getting the money initially.

Make sure you need the money you are attempting to borrow. Sometimes, people borrow money when they could do without it. Owning your business and not having any debt is an enviable position. Ask any business owner.

If you have done the research and found a good lender, and determined the exact amount of money you need in order to go forward, then take a loan. You are the one that knows for sure what you need to make your business happen and to grow it.

C. Using Your Own Cash

Using your own cash is a safe way to start a business. I realize some people just do not have the cash to begin but most of us have some savings. We also have some assets generally that can be turned into cash if the project is worth doing.

Using your own cash is the safest way to go. If you need another desk, wait until you have the cash for it and buy it without using credit. It will take you longer to build your business this way but in the end you will own it all and not have debt. It will give you peace of mind.

Starting out small and building a little at a time can work for many entrepreneurs. If you are in an area where the competition is fierce this may not work for you. Or if your business plan calls for more elaborate surroundings, then a loan may be your only option.

My personal thoughts on taking a loan:

"I have always known I could make the payments if I worked hard enough. Hard work and long hours do not scare me. The challenge has spurred me on at times when the going was rough. I have had passion for my business and that passion drives me to do things I never knew I could accomplish. Real estate is full of challenges and owning a small business is too. Put the two facets together and you have your hands full. There is never a dull moment. There are new challenges every day and every transaction is different. You are constantly learning because of the different aspects of each transaction."

Add agents and staff to the mix, and you have a full time job many times over. You will wear a variety of hats; manager, supervisor, agent, broker, owner, bookkeeper, marketer and the list goes on and on.

I have always been a *"hands on"* person and wanted to know how to do all the tasks necessary in every position in my company. When I first started, this was easy. I was even the janitor at times. Later, however, my company grew and I was forced to delegate jobs to other people. To not know how to do a job myself but trusting someone else to do it, was very difficult. You will realize how much your company has grown when you reach this level. **Delegate. Delegate. Delegate.** It is not easy to do at first but gets easier with time.

Ask yourself, "If I knew my business would grow and would grow rapidly, would I need a loan more now or later?" This is the question to ask. Try to envision your company a year or two from now. Where do you expect it to be? If you take a loan now, will you also need a loan later for expansion and growth? Or is this the time you need it most? These questions should be answered to the best that you can answer without knowing fully what will happen.

There are plateaus in every business. A plateau is a level you reach where you cannot increase the revenue until changes are made in the company. Those changes could be more office space, better equipment, more staff or a variety of other things. You will need money for these changes. An investment from yourself or from loan proceeds will make this occur without taking on partners.

D. PARTNERSHIPS

A partner could be looked at as a 4th option. However, partnerships are difficult and if you have never owned a business before, I suggest you jump right in with both feet and do not take on a partner. You will be learning your own business and it is easier to do this learning by yourself. Partners always move at different speeds. Both have to agree on most things and it can complicate the management of your business. Dealing with a partner can cause so much stress, you lose valuable time and energy to apply to the day to day tasks in your business. *(I learned this lesson the hard way.)*

My first partnership deal:

My partner brought some land to the table. I brought some money. Together, we decided to buy a used doublewide manufactured home, set it up on the lot, tie in utilities (this included installing a septic system since we were in the country). We also had to set a power pole and get it tied into electric service in the area. Fortunately, there was a water line we tapped into and a propane tank provided the fuel for heating. We also had to do any repairs necessary, cleaning and painting, landscape the lot, put it on the market and sell it. We would split the profit equally. It was agreed we would both do the physical work we were capable of to save money.

My partner was not a REALTOR® so I was the one that would sell it and I would charge no commission. She had more land and we planned to do more deals. We thought it was a great partnership.

My learning experience began when I called her the first time to meet me at the home so we could get started with the cleaning and painting we needed to do. She was busy I was informed, and could not come until the next time. As you have guessed, the next time was the next time and the next time. She never got around to coming and doing her part of the work. I learned the hard way. Friendships are not partnerships and should not be considered as such. Get everything in writing and hold each partner accountable.

My money was invested and I needed it back. I knew I could make a profit. So, I was forced to do all the work but that ended what could have been a profitable venture. You must know the person you partner with very well, before you begin or this can happen to you. I thought I knew my partner well, but I did not. I was fortunate to only do one deal with her.

There are many opportunities to make money in real estate not just in commission sales. Being a broker/owner will give you firsthand knowledge that can be converted into profits.

Chapter 6

A. Agents

A few well trained agents vs. all you can hire.

There are pros and cons no matter which way you go. Let's look at both ways. First, a few well trained agents will bring you revenue steadily. Three or four good agents can produce enough to keep your office succeeding but there is a limit to your growth. There are only 24 hours in a day and everyone has to have some time off. Expecting three to four agents to be in the office every day, all day long is not going to happen. There will be times when there will be gaps covering desk duty if you have such a small team.

The upside is knowing that business is being handled efficiently. With a small team, you will be able to communicate with each team member more often and you will know the transactions better and managing is simpler with less people and with people who are trained better. You will have more time to train them too.

If you decide to hire as many agents as you can, your time has been diminished with the sheer number of agents you have to supervise, train, and communicate with daily. There could be more confusion about transactions; less communication means more mistakes.

A lot to weigh here.

More agents mean more money, right? Remember, if there are more agents, there are more expenses. There will be a need for more space, more printing, and you may also experience more squabbles, more noise, more confusion, more chaos, more problems.

However, there may be more money, more transactions, more leads, more listings, more ideas, and more synergy. I guarantee you will have less time to think and make decisions. The fast pace can be fun and exciting but it can also leave you vulnerable to lawsuits. More is a good thing but sometimes it is not the best thing. You will need to decide which kind of agency you want.

There are large franchise real estate companies that subscribe to both of these models I just described. The agencies that hire many agents usually have lots of low producing agents and the smaller ones usually have the top producers. This is not always the case but if you look around your city at the various agencies, you will probably understand better what I am talking about.

If you are considering a franchise, they will lead you in one of these ways. Talking to a franchisor can provide you with valuable information for your area.

In Texas, there are agencies that sponsor one to two thousand agents at a time. An organization like this may have numerous offices and they need designated supervisors in each office. In my experience, the supervision is very lacking in these kinds of agencies. I have often dreaded doing deals with agents from large agencies like this. Most of the work would be done by me and I would actually teach the agents things they should have already learned. These agencies try to provide good training but it is not the same as having a broker/owner in the office daily to advise and guide.

B. Commission Splits

Commission splits is something you rarely hear talked about because agents and brokers are not allowed to discuss commissions on listings but commission splits are different. However, nobody wants someone else to know what kind of money they are making. One of the things I believe hurts so many brokers is giving commission splits that are too large. You have to be able to operate your business in the black and make a living for yourself. Your agents deserve to make a good living too but not if it bankrupts the company!

Offering 70, 80, 90 percent splits is so high most businesses cannot stay in business at that rate but agents expect their brokers to do this for them. Why? Agents rarely have the business in mind when they are negotiating for commission splits. Most are not team oriented or thinking of building your company. They want high commissions, bonuses, incentives, support; they want it all. The trouble with this is most of them do not want to contribute enough of themselves to pay for all of this.

Loyalty plus hard work from a commissioned real estate salesperson can be rare. Competition for good agents is fierce. Be prepared. Owning your own real estate office is about as alone as anyone can be. So, try to build a support team for yourself.

Agents are trained and supported by you and then they can leave over any little thing and go to the competition. Sure, you thought they would never do that. You thought they were interested in building your business and your brand, but guess what! They were only interested in building their business and their brand. Another agency can offer another percent commission or another incentive and they can be history. Don't get your feelings hurt though as you will have to work with them on future transactions that benefit you both, and their new broker.

Yes, the fun has just started. Real estate is a very competitive business. Years ago when I was a newbie someone told me, this business is "dog eat dog."   I did not know what they meant. Within a year, I was well aware of the meaning of that phrase.

I have been disappointed, hurt, shocked and amazed so many times by the actions of an agent I trusted. Today, I approach this differently with caution always and I find that mutual respect and a healthy distance between my agents and me is beneficial. I try to never allow myself to become emotionally vulnerable to any agent or employee. I have had some great people and my team was the best but there was always that healthy distance for my own sake.

Don't let what I have said scare you. It is always best not to mix business and friendship. Find your friends outside of work. Let business be business.

Let the commission splits be fair to both you and your agents. **Making money is why you want to start your own office in the first place.** You are the one taking the risk. The agents only need to show up and produce. Your job is much harder. Do not take your work for granted. Get paid what you deserve as well. With all this said, make the business about serving your client and putting their needs first and the commissions will take care of themselves, if you have the splits right.

Chapter 7

Staff

A. Who answers the phone?

Most real estate companies allow agents to answer the phones. The day is divided into several hourly segments and agents take turns being responsible for answering the phones in the office. The time is known as floor time or desk duty.

When a potential buyer or seller calls the office, the agent on duty will answer the call and try to set an appointment. The buyer or seller will then become that agents' potential client. With a rotating system, every agent has an opportunity to get clients from calls coming into the office. It is the fairest way to share leads. If an agent does not do floor time, they miss leads and usually do not make as much money.

Some agents love floor time and others hate it. If the phones are ringing, agents are happy to spend their time doing this but if the day is slow and the phone rarely rings, the agents become bored and unhappy. There are many ways to spend this time productively but most will not initiate such activities. The broker or sales manager has a responsibility to make sure the agents are making the most of this time. Writing emails, following up with other leads, doing paperwork, studying; all these things can be done in between the phone calls.

In my office, I had a secretary (administrative assistant) who answered the calls. I decided to do this differently from most companies because I have often called other companies and heard all kinds of variations of the "Good morning" message. I like consistency. I like knowing my secretary, only one person, is responsible for getting the call to the right person and getting all the contact information from the caller before they are passed on to an agent. Getting this contact information saved my company lots of money and headaches over the years. We had a good system that worked and I think more companies should do this and their professional image might be enhanced.

Who is Responsible for that?

How many times have you heard someone try to pass the buck and blame someone else for a job that was not finished or completed properly? The best way to avoid this kind of conflict is to have job descriptions that include all the tasks of running your organization and then follow these guidelines. Agents need rules to follow.

B. CHECKLISTS

They need checklists too. It makes their job easier and your job easier also. Use checklists for listings and sales. Using them for buyers and sellers provides contact information and records conversations you and the agents may have with each client. A closing checklist is an efficient way to track all the processes of a transaction during the time between contract signing and closing. During this 4 to 8 week period lots of things are done and lots of conversations are held. The checklist is a diary of this activity. There will be fewer mistakes if you use them and your office will run much more efficiently.

The Texas Association of REALTORS® has a listing checklist in their library that REALTORS® can access. It is a two page document that contains almost everything one could possibly need in a listing. Use this one or make one of your own but use a checklist. It will save you money and possibly a lawsuit.

Wherever you live, the state association should have something similar. If not, check with N.A.R., the National Association of REALTORS®. A listing checklist for sellers will save the office lots of time when it comes time to close a transaction. Having all the documents ahead of time in the file for easy access will make the closing go so much smoother and the title company will not be calling several times a day asking for documents. You will already have them in the file and everyone will be happy.

A closing checklist is vital to meeting deadlines. Making sure you do not miss ordering a survey, inspection or home warranty before closing time. These are just a few of the things you will want to put on this form.

A lot of offices keep files on the computer and this is great but there is always the need for a paper copy as well.   Make sure a hard copy is kept in the office.

The more efficient an office runs the more money you will make. It is as simple as that. Make it easy and take away as much risk as you can.

Your office assistant can make the checklists and supervise the use of them freeing up time for you to do other things. Make sure everyone knows what they are responsible to do. Misunderstandings cost money and morale. Most people do not mind following rules or guidelines as long as they know what to expect. Make a list of expectations for each of your agents and staff. If they do not perform the tasks in the manner you want, they will not be surprised when you have to talk to them about it or they have to find another place to work.

Owning your own office is a challenge in so many ways. You are the boss and "the buck stops here". You may have much more responsibility than you thought you would have when you started but it is also very rewarding in many ways to be the "final word".

If you are up to the challenge, owning your own real estate office and operating it is so much fun. I thoroughly enjoyed my offices. It was never dull or boring. There were new people coming into my life constantly. There were new obstacles with each transaction but also opportunities for growth and learning. Even the problems that will occur on a day to day basis can be challenging and exciting at the same time. If you are competitive and enjoy winning, you will enjoy this profession.

It is not easy especially at first but you can do it! I heard a real estate motivational speaker once say, "This is not rocket science!" That statement meant a lot to me. I would say to myself, I can do this! I can do this! And I did.

Don't let fear keep you from fulfilling your dreams. Don't let friends and family talk you out of trying to be the best you can be. If you have the experience and knowledge it takes to be a broker, have passed your exam, now is the time to step out and take a chance. Learn how to be a motivator, a manager, a recruiter and trainer. Keep your expenses low in the beginning and test the water. You will never know until you try.

I read many years ago that most millionaires will fail, even go bankrupt 2 times before they finally succeed. Not saying you have to try 3 times before you make it but persistence is important. Believing in yourself will make the difference in whether you succeed or not.

When you are the "boss" you are the one that decides the direction of the office. Try a system. If it works, keep it. If it doesn't, try another. You have the right to change things and find what works and what does not. The biggest mistake I ever made was not changing something fast enough. I waited too long expecting things to change and they rarely do. Be

Bold! Make the decisions you need to make as a broker/owner, and make them sooner rather than later.

Who is responsible for that? Ultimately, you are! As a broker/owner you take on all the responsibility of running an office and the responsibility of selling your clients' homes professionally. Any mistakes made will be your responsibility. Listings are also yours. The responsibility a broker takes is huge when you consider every word that comes out of the mouths of their agents is your responsibility. Even when they don't speak; the things they do not say, they should have said are your responsibility. Omissions are treated the same as Commissions. Said or not said, done or not done.   Mistakes happen and you will deal with each one.

If you are looking at this right now and thinking "I can't do this", remember how many brokers and owners are operating successful offices right now. Do not be scared. Your office can be just as successful. The opportunity is there and now is the time! Go for it!

C. Policies and Procedures

Today in Texas, every office must have a policies and procedures manual. It is mandatory. You can be fined for not having one. With the new broker responsibility laws, policies and procedures is the new way of supervising agents and informing them of office procedures. I required all new agents and staff to read the entire book and sign it, to acknowledge they had read it and understood what it said. It was not difficult reading and it informed new recruits how things would be handled in our office. It actually saved time in the long run. It also limited problems and possible lawsuits from occurring. When everyone is on the same page and knows what to expect, things will run smoother.

I think every office should have **Errors and Omissions** Insurance. This insurance can protect an office from frivolous lawsuits and keep you in business. I like to do business with offices that practice professionalism and this is one marker of a professional office, in my opinion. Not all offices have E & O insurance. In fact, most do not. The problem with that is if a lawsuit occurs because of a negligent agent in another office that cooperated on a transaction with your office, your office may be brought into the lawsuit whether your agent did anything wrong or not.

T.A.R., the Texas Association of REALTORS® and the Texas Real Estate Commission are doing a study right now concerning Errors and Omissions Insurance. It may become mandatory in the future for every office to have it. This would please me but there will be many offices that will fight such a ruling.   It is another expense you should prepare for when you open your office.

For a new broker, I highly recommend getting the insurance, especially if you are going to hire agents. Every word they speak can be a liability for you. You cannot supervise them all day long and at night too. You will not be going out on listing appointments or showing appointments with them either. They have lots of opportunities to say the wrong thing while with a client.

Policies and Procedures manuals entail so many things and I cannot discuss every one of those in this book. I do want to touch on some of the things I feel are most important. One of those things is **Fair Housing**. I trained my agents every week during our sales meetings but I held two special meetings each year to talk about Fair Housing only. The Federal laws concerning Fair Housing should be something every agent is fully aware of and practices easily. No discrimination because of race, color, national origin, familial status, sexual orientation or religion is allowed. A broker is responsible to make sure discrimination does not happen in their office or with any client their agents are working with.

This is a zero tolerance policy that must be adhered to and never taken lightly.

Note: E & O insurance will not cover you if you break the law and this is law.

Policies and Procedures can describe systems of doing the paperwork, dress codes, hours of operation, use of company equipment and supplies, training, meetings, image of the company and so many other things. You may obtain a generic policy and procedures guide from your local association or you may write one of your own. I also add to mine when I find new information that fits. Either way, having one in Texas is a must. In other states it may not be mandatory but it is wise to have one. It makes things easier and the easier your office operates, the more money you will make.

I had a **weekly sales meeting** and I also **trained my agents** during this time. **Testing your agents** occasionally on their knowledge of certain subjects is wise. I had a competency quiz that I gave my agents once a year. I wanted to know their level of competency and any areas they needed to improve on. Using role play is an excellent way to train. Agents may not like it at first but once they get used to it, they thoroughly enjoy it and learn faster than conventional book study.

In my office I used job descriptions for every position and that included the agents. There was a list of expectations for them as well as for the staff. If an agent was not willing to work hard and bring something of value to the office, we did not need them. You will find many people with real estate licenses that just want a place where they can come several times a week and drink coffee and hang out and talk. A successful office needs to not hire these kinds of agents but if you get one, weed them out quickly. Otherwise, they will ruin others. You need people who are dedicated to the office and want to be a part of something that grows and succeeds. When you have these kinds of agents, you will be unstoppable. Do not waste your time with the others. You can spend lots of money on agents that take up desk space, use supplies, lose clients and bring down the morale in the office. Let these agents go to another office, the sooner, the better.

A long time ago, I had an agent like this. She was super intelligent and had lots of potential but the attitude she displayed was not always good. She had a chip on her shoulder. She had some hard times in her life and I felt sorry for her and knew she was trying to overcome these situations in her life. One day she was great and the next day she was a different person altogether.

One problem I had with her was the constant questioning of me in sales meetings. Things she should ask in private were brought up in front of all the agents. A few times did not bother me but after a while, it became almost confrontational.

Then, there were times when I walked into an office and she and several others were talking and the talking would stop. I knew things were getting worse. I should have fired her then but I waited and hoped things would get better. I tried private discussions with her but to no avail. In the end, she cost me three other agents. This is why I say, cut these kinds of people quickly from your employ. They are a cancer and will destroy your business.

She went to the competition and continued her assaults. Two more agencies and now she is no longer an agent.

These kinds of agents always end up out of the business eventually but you do not want your office to be a statistic because you did not fire quickly enough. Take this lesson from me. I have learned it well.

CHAPTER 8

Expert Recommendations

When starting your business, you will have so many questions that pop up every day. Some of these things are questions you have already answered. Some of them, however, are not. Where do you get the answers you need?

Go to the experts in the field. Depending on the questions, there are people you know locally that can answer most of the questions you have.

If it is financing, go to your **local banker**. If it is advertising, inquire at the **newspaper office or magazines** for your area. **Marketing experts** are expensive to hire but with a little research, you can find what works for you and what does not. Don't get tied up in lengthy contracts, especially with online advertising. If it has to do with financial planning, make an appointment with a good **CPA**. They will have lots of answers for you.

If you need some leadership skills, motivation, time management training, sales development; I'd like to recommend Brian Tracy and his books.

A. Brian Tracy

Brian Tracy is an international best-selling author, business counsellor and success strategist. He has written many best-selling books on business and sales, and is recognized as a business leader.

I have read many of his books and tried to apply what I learned over the years. I cannot stress how important it is to listen to people who have the experience you may lack. Brian Tracy is an author you will want to become familiar with if you have not already.

Brian has books that are easy to understand and many have step by step applications.   When you read his books, it is like he is talking to you directly. This is the secret to his success.

I believe Brian's advice to you would be to never stop learning. Real estate is one of those professions that demand you never stop learning. Brian's books on increasing sales will help you and your agents. He will help you make and achieve your goals, increase productivity and creativity. He will explain the psychology of success. These are things not taught in real estate school. You have to learn this outside continuing education. Brian Tracy is a good resource and a great motivator.

B. Pat Strong

Pat Strong is a Texas Real Estate Commission Certified instructor. She holds these designations, ABR, ABRM, CRB, E-Pro, GRI, SRS, SRES, AHWD, CNHS, RFS, SFR, TAHS, ECO BROKER, CREI, TAR Senior Instructor, TAR "ITI" Instructor, 2006 TAR Educator of the Year, 2009 REBAC Hall of Fame.

She teaches a variety of classes to real estate agents across the state and has taught in other states as well. I asked her to share her thoughts on what she thinks the most important things are that someone should consider when first opening their own office. This is what she said.

"When opening an office, there are many considerations as follows:

What is my goal/purpose for owning my own company?

Do I have a short term/long term business plan?

Will this be a virtual office or bricks and mortar office?

Do I have enough contacts in my "book of business" to immediately begin doing business?

As a broker/owner, how many agents do I want to be responsible for in my office?

Do I personally have the money to set up and sustain this office for the time it will take to be profitable?

Do I have the patience I need to own, operate, maintain, be a leader and train agents?

If I choose not to train agents myself, what career path will I place these agents on?

Will I choose not to have any agents or will I choose to only recruit agents who are seasoned?

Benefits of owning and operating are: It is your business solely, excitement of growing your business and becoming profitable, being the leader of a team of agents to become successful and if done properly, something to pass to heirs or sell and retire.

These questions are just a tip of the "iceberg" and much planning and thinking must be done prior to this new venture."

These are Pat Strongs' thoughts and as you can see this book deals with all these things. Getting advice from someone like Pat is invaluable. Pat has been my friend for many years and I have attended many of her classes. I highly recommend her classes to anyone wanting more education in any area of the real estate field. Pat is a great teacher and she is always knowledgeable of new changes within the industry.

If you need more real estate courses or just continuing education, I recommend Pat Strong. She teaches classes in Texas. You can find her classes by going to www.stronginstructor.com

Do not be afraid to ask advice from experts. Most people will feel honored that you asked for their help. They have experience that can make your way much easier. Pat Strong is one of those people. She is not only a good friend but a very valuable resource.

If you are located outside of Texas, spend time with local instructors. They can be a real help.

C. Legal Advice

In Texas, real estate brokers that are members of the Texas Association of Realtors have a **legal hotline** available to them. This has come in handy many times in the past for me. It is a free service and if you can wait until the next day for an answer, someone will call you. This is almost as good as having a paid attorney on retainer.

Your own **personal attorney** is usually a must as well. There are times when certain kinds of contracts need to be written and you need an attorney for that. Often disputes with other brokers, agents or clients will be cause for your own attorney. Plan this expense in your budget.

Another great source for advice is your **local title companies**. Title companies love to help agents with title questions. Many times, they have helped me and there is no fee for their help. I try to use the title companies that provide help to questions that are hard for agents to answer as often as possible. They have lots of information at their disposal we do not have. I can get land restrictions, HOA regulations, old surveys on file from them and so much more. Having good title companies that like working with you is such a benefit for any office.

Title companies also have an attorney on hand for legal questions. Most of these companies will also take time to come to your office for short training periods for your agents. Title companies can provide many valuable hours of help to your office.

I hope you enjoyed some of the stories I have shared with you in this book. I tell them to you so that you might avoid bad situations in your office or to give you some inspiration. While deciding which stories would benefit you most, one came to mind. This is very important. It doesn't deal with opening your office but is a problem that many agents face from time to time.

I went on a listing appointment one day. The house had been previously listed for a year and a half with another agency. The owner had no idea why it had not sold. I viewed the home and it was very clean, well maintained, appealing to the eye and there was no obvious reason why it had not sold. As we were discussing matters and doing paperwork, I asked about the title. The owner was recently widowed; for just a couple years.

I asked her about her husbands' death and listened to her story. I showed empathy and spent the time with her that was needed before asking the hard questions. Then I asked if he had a will. She quickly said yes, and told me the house belonged to her. They bought the home together and there were no children. The home had been willed to her.

I then asked if she had the will probated and if I could see the paperwork. She told me she had not had the will probated. I could not believe it. This home was listed for a year and a half by another agency and the will was not probated. That meant it was still in both her name and her husband's name. Not a clear title!

The other agent had not told her it was necessary. She questioned me wondering if I knew what I was talking about. A quick call to the title company assured her I did.

We immediately set up an appointment with an attorney to get the will probated. It took six weeks start to finish. We were rushing the attorney and the court to get it done. In a bigger city, it could have taken three to six months.

Little did we know at the time, we would get a cash buyer. They wanted immediate possession. We closed the day after the title was cleared! Our title company was so good working to coordinate everything with the probate attorney to make a quick closing even possible.

So, teach your agents about probate and make sure the title is clear before they try to sell the houses. It will save you time and headaches.

This is an example of how title companies and attorneys are your go-to experts. They work together to help you help your clients.

If you have questions about anything concerning transactions or your business, find an expert. If you have to pay for their advice, do it. It will save you time and money always.

Another old saying I love is: **"Better safe, than sorry."**

Chapter 9

The BIG Decisions

When I began this book, I looked back at my almost forty year career in real estate and thought, "what would I have wanted to know in the beginning when I started my first office? What advice would I have profited from the most, if someone had been willing to share with me their experiences and knowledge?"

These few chapters contain some of the most valuable advice I can give you. They certainly do not cover everything you will need to know but they may give you some insight into what approaches you need to take in the startup of your new office. **Having asked the right questions, you are closer to finding the right answers for yourself.**

A. Why, What, Where, How & When

Take time to answer **"The Why"** and this will help you in those hard moments you will most likely have especially during the first year. Most small businesses fail in the first year or two of operation but with good planning they do not have to. The answer to "The Why" will keep you focused and prevent you from giving up too soon.

The rewards that can be measured and those that cannot are both important, but the numbers are the **bottom line**. Don't overlook the numbers. **Track your numbers.** Leads, appointments, client retention, closings and follow up all need to be measured. These numbers will equal dollars in the bank.

Don't overlook **"the What, the Where, the How and the When".** Deciding on starting a new office or buying a pre-existing office can be a hard decision. Depending on your age, your location, your experience, the opportunities available, the money you have to invest, and other factors, the decision might actually turn out to be simple. Either way, it is a big decision and you must look at all possibilities.

Branding and marketing is one thing you need to spend lots of time planning as it is what you will spend most of your money on. Advertising can make your business visible to the public quickly, it can bring clients through the door but it cannot give them the service they need. So advertising is necessary, but well trained dedicated agents will make your business a success.

Recognition from business owners is important as you are building a reputation in the community. This reputation will hurl you toward success and will speak for you when you are not there to speak for yourself. This reputation will open doors for you without extra effort. It is the intangible that has no cost but is immeasurable in value.

In Chapter 3 we discussed the ideal location. Location is important in real estate and finding that special place and staying there is also important. In this business, clients usually return to the agents and the office that helped them buy their home, when they are ready to sell it. Being at the same location can mean the difference in whether you have repeat business from some clients. People do not like following businesses to different locations. You may be able to move once or even twice during the operation of your business, but you should know it will cost you many dollars when you move. So choose your location wisely in the beginning.

A Business Plan can help you obtain the funding you will need to start up your own office. It will serve as your guide to help you stay on a planned course of action. Time spent in planning and preparation is never a waste.

Write down your goals. **Analyze your performance often and be flexible** when you need to be flexible. I think lots of people hesitate when writing goals because they fear they will not be able to change those goals in midstream. Nothing is farther from the truth. Being flexible means being able to make changes, and that will improve your success many times over.

Using your own cash is always the best way to go. Getting out of debt and staying out of debt is the new American Dream. As a new business owner, this might not be possible, so we have discussed banks and private lenders, even partnerships to obtain the cash you will need to start your own office. Don't underestimate this amount. It will always be more than what you thought it would be. Have different options available before you need them if more cash is needed. **Not planning for the unexpected is a sure fire way to fail.**

Agents can be the lifeblood of your agency or they can squeeze every drop out of you. You must protect yourself and your business from agents who will waste your time and your resources. Their concern is for themselves and their paychecks more than for the health of your business. Never forget this.

Brokers need to spend time training and supervising agents but they have much more to do than this. Spending too much time with agents is as bad a practice as not spending enough time with them. Find the balance.

You need a good support network to discuss everything from expenses to transactions. That network is not in your office. You are the management now. You are not part of the workforce in your office anymore. Making this transition requires a change of mind in many areas of your business.

If you have been an agent for many years and now you are stepping into the broker/owner's shoes, those shoes are much different. You cannot continue to think like an agent.

The responsibility you are undertaking is huge and the profit or loss will be all yours.

The first contact a potential client has with your office is usually what the client will use to measure the service they will receive from your agency. First impressions are most important. Make sure it is a positive message that comes across to your potential clients.

Checklists will save your office time and money. They will make things run smoother and more efficiently.

Order a policies and procedures manual or write one before you even open the front door of your office. Following the steps outlined in this book will help you be more successful and get your office up and running faster.

I wish you success in all your endeavors and hope this book helps you to avoid making some of the mistakes I have made over the years. An ounce of prevention, my Mom used to say, is worth a pound of cure!

B. Client Communication

"Old School" vs. High Tech

Here is one more question for you to ponder. Old School or High Tech? What does this mean? To me, "Old School" refers to the way things used to be done and High Tech is the modern way of thinking and doing. It is much more than that. "Old School" taught us to value client relationships, and face to face conversations brought more success. Is that still true today? I believe it is. Many may disagree with me but I've tried it both ways. Personal contact verses computer and digital contact; I find I spend less time and have fewer mistakes and unhappy clients when I use more personal contacts than computerized. **Communication is the key to success. The better we communicate, the more money we make.** When the communication between parties is good, we have fewer disagreements, the negotiations are better, and the transactions are smoother.

Obviously, I prefer the "Old School" ways but I use all the modern technology I can to make my life easier. I do not buy leads, however. Maybe you do and maybe they work for you. I hope they work if you spend all that money on lead purchases. I prefer to target market and this works better for me. I can saturate an area or a group of people and spend more time with each one, making personal contacts rather than just texting or emailing. We can become so busy these days, we can forget that having a personal face to face conversation with a potential client can help discover motivations, wants and needs, which will definitely make you money faster. A five minute conversation like this can be much more helpful than 10 to 20 emails over a period of a week. Save time. Go see your potential clients. Knock on their door, buy them a cup of coffee, take them to lunch. You will find these "Old School" ways will pay off faster than buying a new Tablet or gadget.

There are many classes you can attend that teach body language. If you have never taken a class on body language, it is well worth the time and money you will spend on such a class. Learn what hand gestures, facial expressions and body shifting mean when talking to a client. **Discovering a client's motivation is the absolute most important thing you need to know in any transaction. Body language will tell you those motivations faster than anything else.**

To read body language you must have face to face conversations. Now you understand why I prefer personal conversations to emails and texts. I like to get the transaction going and sold as fast as I can.

I have heard agents talk about spending weeks, months and even years with clients. I want to ask them why? Obviously, anyone spending months or years with a client has not listened or understood their buyer's needs. Otherwise, they would have been able to help their clients purchase the kind of property they were looking for.

It is important to teach these principles to your agents as well. You cannot stay in business if you don't make the sales.

Agents that spend too much time with a client before they make the sale are not practicing these principles. I want happy clients and they are happier when I help them find the property they are looking for and get it bought or help them sell their property so they can move on with their plans.

How important is body language? *One day one of my agents came to me and told me about a couple she had been showing homes to. The lady was very nice but her husband was gruff and she could not seem to win his favor in anything she said or did. My agent was very frustrated. She felt she was going around and around and not making any headway with these buyers.*

She asked me if I would meet them and talk for a bit and give her some pointers as to how to proceed. I willingly agreed.

The next day the buyers came into the office and we offered them some coffee in the conference room. I went in after they were seated and introduced myself. I began to ask them what they were looking for in regards to a new home. It was the usual chit chat and vague answers.

I knew this conversation was going nowhere. So, I sat there for a moment or two quietly. I looked down; I fiddled with my *papers. It was almost embarrassing for the quiet was lasting so long. When I finally spoke, I had everyone's attention. I looked at the man and said, "My agent has been trying to find you a house, but she is lost as to what you REALLY are looking for.* **Can you, will you tell me?***

He sat there quietly as well. We looked each other in the eye for the longest and finally he said, "Yes, I will tell you."

He asked if he and I could talk alone. I said, "Yes." We walked into my office and shut the door. Then he shared with me his health problems and prognosis. He had been gruff and sometimes hateful with my agent. He was in pain. He had cancer and he did not have much time left.

He wanted a home where he could feel his wife was safe and secure. He wanted a home with very little maintenance. He wanted things to be easy for his wife to care for later when he was gone.

Now, things were put into perspective. We discussed all the possibilities available for him and price ranges comfortable for their situation. That week we found this couple their perfect retirement home.

Closing was fast. We worked with a great title company and we had all the documents quickly drawn up and closing occurred within two weeks. They were very happy.

Furniture arrived on time. They were busy meeting new neighbors and within a couple more weeks they had friends dropping by. We checked on them several times to see how things were going.

Sadly to say, the gentleman passed away within a few weeks of moving in. His wife was set though. He had accomplished what he needed to do for her. She was happy to be there and to be settled; having friends close by helped.

My agent learned a good lesson. Sometimes, when clients are fussy, they have things on their mind we cannot imagine. When we know their TRUE MOTIVATION for buying, the process is much easier. His body language told me he wanted to tell someone what was bothering him but he did not know how. I gave him the opportunity to tell me.

C. You Are The Boss

You may have heard that old saying "The Buck Stops Here". I heard it many times while I was growing up. It originated from the dealing of cards; but President Truman back in the 1940's had a sign on his desk saying the same thing. He said what it meant to him was that if a decision needed to be made, he was the one that would have to make it. No one else was in line after him. So, when you own and operate your own office, you are the boss and the buck stops here.

No one else will take responsibility for the decisions you make. Liability comes with responsibility. When a decision needs to be made, who can you turn to for advice if the buck stops here?

Good real estate attorneys are nice to have close by. Problems can arise with every deal and having someone to call is often necessary. Title companies are also a good source for information. Remember, your state associations of Realtors® also have attorneys on call for our use.

Call someone when you have problems arise. If you do not feel comfortable making a decision when you have little experience in that area or if you have limited knowledge, call the experts. They are there to help you.

It's time to make that decision to step out or not.

Make the decision.

Don't just put it off until there is no decision to be made.

Consciously, decide. Are you ready?

Is it time for you to be

"Finally A Broker!"